FRIENDS

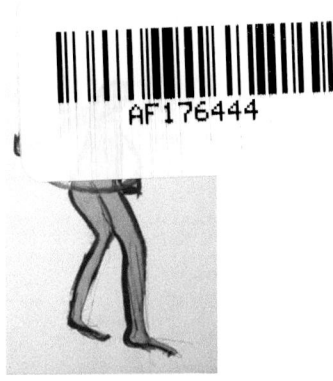

AF176444

An English play in 9 scenes about FRIENDS

For Years 3, 4 and 5 (Level 2/1)

By John Middleton

Bibliografische Information der Deutschen Nationalbibliothek:
Die Deutsche Nationalbibliothek verzeichnet diese Publikation in der Deutschen Nationalbibliografie; detaillierte bibliografische Daten sind im Internet über http://dnb.dnb.de abrufbar.

© 2020 John Middleton

United States Copyright Office

1-8759744361

Herstellung und Verlag: BoD – Books on Demand, Norderstedt

ISBN: 9783751917445

Other plays from THE PLAYLET SERIES by John Middleton:

EVERY DAY – a play in 10 scenes about EVERYDAY LIFE
for Years 2, 3 and 4 (Level 1/1)

NEW KEY CHAIN – a play in 15 scenes about KEYS
for Years 6, 7 and 8 (Level 3/1)

LUCKY CHARMS – a play in 10 scenes about LUCK
for Years 6, 7 and 8 (Level 3/2)

STAND UP – a play in 8 scenes about MORAL COURAGE
for Years 8, 9 and 10 (Level 4/1)

FEAR – a play in 7 scenes about FEAR
for Years 9, 10 and 11 (Level 5/1)

MONOLOGS FOR YOUNG ADULTS – 25 scenes
for Years 11 and 12 or for university students (September 2020)

FSC

www.fsc.org

MIX

Papier aus ver-
antwortungsvollen
Quellen

Paper from
responsible sources

FSC® C105338

<u>**CONTENTS**</u>

Jonathan – Tony's classmate
Cooper – Tony's classmate
Mike – Tony's classmate
Ed – Tony's classmate
Sarah – Tony's classmate
Angelina – Tony's classmate
Ariane – Tony's classmate
Jackie – Tony's classmate
Pia – Tony's classmate
Taylor – Tony's sister

Scene 8   YOU CAN DO IT
Rudolfo – a boy
Victoria – a classmate
Giselle – a classmate
Courtney – a classmate
Dave – a classmate
Steve – a classmate

Scene 9   I'M SORRY
Riley – a girl who is angry
Lilly – Riley's ex-girlfriend
Dakota – Riley's classmate
Jamey – Riley's classmate
Tom – Riley's classmate
Jason – Riley's classmate

FOREWORD

FRIENDS is a play for advanced elementary students in Years 4, 5, or 6 (Level 2/1). It is designed for a normal-sized English class and for students with varying interests in acting. Since there are 42 roles – none of which are really minor – students who enjoy acting can perform in several scenes and play to their heart's content, whereas students who aren't particularly keen on acting only have one role to master in one single scene. Every scene deals with the general topic of friendship, the hope, the fun, the disappointment and the anger connected with finding, keeping and losing friends. The themes are geared to the experiences of students today and offer young actresses and actors the opportunity to discover a wide variety of feelings while performing. The plots are believable and understandable, the language is idiomatic and easily accessible for English learners. FRIENDS works well when performed for smaller audiences: parents and other classes. But it can also be highly entertaining for a large audience. Performing time: about one hour. Of course, it is also possible to select individual scenes and perform them as simple skits outside the context of FRIENDS. In that case it is still recommendable to create a suitable setting for presenting the skits to an audience. The true joy of performing a foreign-language play is to feel it click, to realize that the people watching the performance don't only "get the picture", they are also delighted to see a story come to life when presented in English by non-native performers.

– John Middleton, Hamburg, 2020

SCENE 1   MY BEST FRIEND

(Oscar is sitting on a bench – stage right. He has something on his lap, but we can't see what it is. He is talking to it.)

OSCAR

Hey, Charlie, I have an idea. Let's go to the playground and swing.

CHARLIE *(Oscar changes his voice and talks for Charlie)*

Oh, that's a good idea, Oscar.

OSCAR

And afterwards we can get some ice cream.

CHARLIE *(Oscar changes his voice and talks for Charlie)*

Ice cream? I love ice cream, Oscar.

OSCAR

Strawberry ice cream is the best, isn't it?

CHARLIE *(Oscar changes his voice and talks for Charlie)*

Yes, you're right, Oscar. Strawberry is always the best.

OSCAR *(picks up a puppet that was lying on his lap – it is Charlie)*

Do you know what, Charlie?

CHARLIE *(Oscar turns the puppet to look at him and changes his voice)*

What, Oscar?

OSCAR

I'm glad you're my friend.

CHARLIE *(Oscar changes his voice and talks for Charlie)*

And I'm glad you're my friend.

OSCAR

And when the other kids come, you won't play with them, will you?

CHARLIE *(Oscar changes his voice and talks for Charlie)*

No, I won't play with the other kids, because you're my friend, Oscar.

OSCAR

I don't really have any friends, because friends are stupid… EXCEPT FOR YOU. You are my only friend, Charlie.

CHARLIE *(Oscar changes his voice and talks for Charlie)*

And you're my only friend, too, Oscar.

OSCAR

You always want to do what I do, and you never say I'm wrong, and you're always on my side. Not like that stupid Ron I used to play with.

CHARLIE *(Oscar changes his voice and talks for Charlie)*

I thought Ron was one of your best friends.

OSCAR

Not anymore. Hey, Charlie. Who's this?

(Oscar holds one hand up in the air and wiggles his fingers. Then his hand moves downward and starts to tickle Charlie.)

CHARLIE *(Oscar changes his voice and talks for Charlie who starts jumping around)*

Oh no, it's Mr. Tickle.

CHARLIE *(Oscar changes his voice and laughs for Charlie)*

Ha, ha, ha.

(Larry and Ron appear – stage left. Oscar sees them and looks away.)

LARRY *(looking at Oscar who is tickling Charlie)*

Hey, Ron, isn't that Oscar over there?

RON

Yeah.

LARRY

What's he doing?

RON

It looks like he's tickling his puppet.

LARRY

His puppet?

RON

Yeah, he has a puppet named Charlie. We used to be good friends, but now he says that Charlie is his only friend.

LARRY

Oh really?

RON

He talks for Charlie, and they do stuff together. It's weird. How can a puppet be a friend? Puppets aren't alive. They can't talk and do stuff on their own.

LARRY

I don't think it's so stupid.

(Larry pulls a puppet out of his backpack.)

RON

What's that?

LARRY

This is one of my best friends, Willy.

RON

You have a puppet, too?

LARRY

Willy, say hi to Ron.

WILLY *(Larry changes his voice and talks for Willy)*

Hi, Ron. Nice to meet you.

RON *(looks confused)*

Hi… Willy.

(Larry holds up Willy's hand, and Ron hesitantly shakes it.)

RON

Hey there.

WILLY *(Larry changes his voice and talks for Willy)*

You know, Ron, Larry has told me lots of things about you.

RON

Oh yeah?

WILLY *(Larry changes his voice and talks for Willy)*
Yeah. He says you're one of his best friends.
RON
Well, he's one of my best friends, too.
WILLY *(Larry changes his voice and talks for Willy)*
Great. He's really a nice guy.
(Willy looks up.)
Oh look, there's Charlie! *(yelling)* Hello, Charlie! How are you doing?
(Larry holds up Willy and helps him wave. Oscar holds up Charlie and helps him wave, too.)
CHARLIE *(Oscar changes his voice and talks for Charlie)*
Hi, Willy!
WILLY *(Larry changes his voice and talks for Willy)*
Come on over here. I want you to meet my new friend, Ron.
CHARLIE *(Oscar changes his voice and talks for Charlie)*
Okay, I'm coming.
OSCAR *(to Willy)*
What are you doing? You know Ron and I aren't friends anymore.
CHARLIE *(to Oscar)*
Aw, come on, Oscar. Willy's my good friend. Let's go over there.
OSCAR *(to Charlie)*
I really don't want to, but you're my best friend, so I'll do it for you.
(Oscar walks over to the others with Charlie.)
RON
Hi, Charlie. Nice to see you.
CHARLIE *((Oscar changes his voice and talks for Charlie)*
Hi, Ron. You know Oscar, don't you?

RON

Yeah, I know him. We used to be friends a long time ago.

(Oscar glares at him.)

WILLY *(Larry changes his voice and talks for Willy)*

Hey, Charlie, do you know my best friend Larry?

CHARLIE *(Oscar changes his voice and talks for Charlie)*

Yes, I think I've seen him before. Hi, Larry.

LARRY

Hi, Charlie. Hi, Oscar.

OSCAR

Hi.

WILLY *(Larry changes his voice and talks for Willy)*

Hey, I have a good idea.

CHARLIE *(Oscar changes his voice and talks for Charlie)*

What's that?

WILLY *(Larry changes his voice and talks for Willy)*

We can all go to Larry's house. It's his sister's birthday, and we can put on a puppet show for her. She just turned five today.

CHARLIE *(Oscar changes his voice and talks for Charlie)*

That's a great idea.

LARRY

Oh yeah, Susie would really love a puppet show. It's her birthday today, but she's sick and can't have a party. She would be thrilled if we put on a puppet show for her.

WILLY *(to Ron, Larry changes his voice and talks for Willy)*

Would you like to come, too, Ron?

RON

I'm not sure. I don't have a puppet, and I've never put on a puppet show before.

CHARLIE *(Oscar changes his voice and talks for Charlie)*
No problem, Ron. Oscar has another puppet in his backpack. I'm sure he'd lend it to you.
(Oscar and Ron look at each other. Suddenly Oscar smiles, and Ron smiles, too.
RON *(to Oscar)*
Is that right, Oscar? Do you have another puppet?
OSCAR
Sure. His name is Georgie. And you know what?
RON
What?
OSCAR
He remembers you.
RON
He does?
OSCAR
Yes, he asked about you last week.
RON
Oh really.
OSCAR
If you like, you can borrow Georgie.
RON
That's great. I've never had a puppet before.
(Oscar gives Georgie to Ron.)
RON
Thanks, Oscar.
OSCAR
You're welcome, Ron.
CHARLIE *(Oscar changes his voice and talks for Charlie)*
Hey, I have a great idea for the puppet show. I'll tell you guys about it on the way to Larry's house.
(The three boys and their puppets walk off stage.)

SCENE 2   IS THERE ANYTHING I CAN DO?

(Jenny walks on stage. It looks like she has been crying, because she has her face in her hands. Another girl, Sarah, quickly joins Jenny.)

SARAH

Jenny, what's wrong? Why are you crying? Is there a problem?

(Jenny wipes her eyes and nods her head.)

SARAH

Is there anything I can do?

(Jenny shakes her head, then wipes her eyes again.)

SARAH

Did somebody say something to hurt you?

(Jenny nods.)

SARAH

Was it Matilda?

(Jenny nods.)

SARAH

That girl is so mean. I don't believe it.

(Jenny nods.)

SARAH

What did she say this time?

(Jenny tugs at her dress.)

SARAH

She said something about your dress?

(Jenny nods.)

SARAH

Hey, come on. You can tell me. We're friends forever.

(Sarah holds out her hand, and Jenny slowly holds out her hand. Then they shake hands in a very special way.)

JENNY

She came up to me…

SARAH

And then?

JENNY

She came up to me when I was alone and said, "I love your dress."

SARAH

And then?

JENNY

Later when I was standing with some other girls outside, she said, "Oh Jenny, where did you get that dress? It looks just like the rag we clean the floors with. It must be secondhand. Or did your Mommy make it for you?"

SARAH

And then?

JENNY

She laughed and said to the other girls, "I'd stay away from that stupid girl. She's a real loser!"

SARAH

Matilda is the meanest girl I know.

JENNY

And you know what really hurts, Sarah?

SARAH

What?

JENNY

Matilda is my next-door neighbor. We used to be best friends. She knows all about me.

SARAH

Then why did she talk about your mom? She knows your mom died last year, doesn't she?

JENNY

Sure, she and her family were at the funeral.

SARAH

So she just talks about your mom to hurt you?

(Jenny nods.)

SARAH

It's time somebody put Matilda in her place.

JENNY

What are you going to do?

(At that moment, we hear Matilda laughing. She appears on stage with Johanna.)

MATILDA

Just wait and see.

(Matilda and Johanna start walking past Jenny and Sarah.)

MATILDA *(to Johanna)*

Then I told her it looked like the rag we cleaned the floors with.

JOHANNA *(stops laughing, sees Jenny and Sarah)*

Oh yeah?

MATILDA

Actually, her Mommy probably made it for her.

JOHANNA *(stops walking)*

And what's wrong with that? My mom makes lots of stuff for me, too.

(Matilda stops walking and looks back at Johanna. Sarah and Jenny have stopped talking and are listening to Matilda and Johanna.)

MATILDA *(to Johanna)*

Don't you understand? Her mom's dead!

JOHANNA

I don't understand what you're talking about.

MATILDA *(getting angry)*

Jenny thinks she's so cool, 'cause her mom died. She thinks she's so special, but she's such a loser! Just look at those ugly dresses she wears! She only wears them, 'cause her mother made them. She has no idea how stupid she looks. Like a grandmother or something.

(*At that moment, Sarah walks in front of Matilda.*)

SARAH

Hold on, Matilda! I heard what you said, and I don't like it.

MATILDA (surprised)

What do you mean?

SARAH

I heard what you said about Jenny.

MATILDA (*looks at Jenny*)

Oh, you mean that loser over there.

SARAH

She's no loser. She's a great girl.

MATILDA

Says who?

SARAH

Says me.

JOHANNA

And me, too.

MATILDA (*to Johanna*)

Hey Johanna, are you taking sides with Jenny?

JOHANNA

I don't think you're being fair to Jenny. She's a nice girl, and she's had…

MATILDA

You're supposed to be on my side, Johanna, because you're my best friend!

JOHANNA

I'm sorry, Matilda, even if I am your best friend, I can think for myself. And I think you're wrong.

MATILDA

You think I'm wrong?

JOHANNA

Yes, it's wrong to say the things you said about Jenny.

MATILDA

If that's what you think, then you're a loser, too!

JOHANNA

If that's what you think, then you're a loser, too, because you just lost me as your best friend.

MATILDA

What did you just say?

JOHANNA

I said you're a loser, because you just lost me. Goodbye, Matilda.

(Matilda is very angry. She turns around and runs away.)

MATILDA

I hate all of you.

(Johanna walks over to Jenny.)

SARAH

Wow, that was cool.

JOHANNA

Hey Jenny, I'm sorry about what Matilda said to you.

(Jenny nods.)

JENNY

Thanks for standing up for me, Johanna.

JOHANNA

Nobody should ever treat you like that, Jenny. That wasn't fair.

(Johanna and Jenny smile at each other.)

SARAH

Hey guys, I have to go. I'll call you later, Jenny.

JENNY

Yeah, thanks for everything, Sarah.

SARAH

Friends forever, Jenny.

JENNY

Friends forever, Sarah.

(Jenny and Sarah do their special handshake.)

JOHANNA *(still looking at Jenny)*

What are you doing now?

JENNY

I have to go to the library.

JOHANNA

That's funny. I was just going to the library myself.

JENNY

Then we can go there together.

JOHANNA

Great idea. And afterwards we can get some ice cream
at that new ice cream shop next to the library.

JENNY

Wonderful idea.

(Jenny and Johanna walk off stage together.)

SCENE 3   CAN I TRUST YOU?

(Mia and her neighbor Scarlet are sitting at the kitchen table at Mia's house. Scarlet is wearing strange-looking clothes, and she has a funny hair-do.)

SCARLET

Listen, Mia, I have to take a little trip this morning. Could you run over to my house and feed my Boogalooga in about an hour? Its food is on the table.

MIA

Sure, Scarlet. I'd love to.

SCARLET

Thanks, Mia. You're a big help.

MIA

Where are you going?

SCARLET *(puts her index finger to her lips)*

Top secret. I'll tell you when I get back.

MIA *(smiles)*

Okay.

SCARLET

Have I ever told you how great it is to have a nice neighbor like you?

MIA

Well, you're the best neighbor I've ever had and the most unusual.

SCARLET

I certainly am unusual, aren't I?

MIA

I just wish I could tell my girlfriend Emily about you.

SCARLET

If you want to, you can.

MIA

Really? That's great.

SCARLET

I mean, she probably won't believe you, but just in case she does believe you, you must make her forget your secret again.

MIA

How do I do that?

SCARLET

Just put your left hand on her right shoulder and say: May this secret be silent forever.

MIA

And then she'll forget what I told her?

SCARLET

Completely.

(Scarlet gets up.)

So, I have to be going now. See you later.

MIA

Have a good trip.

SCARLET

And give the Boogalooga two drops of water and one drop of milk to drink.

MIA

I will. See you later.

(Scarlet exits. Emily enters.)

EMILY

Hi, Mia, your neighbor Scarlet let me in.

MIA

Oh, you just ran into her? That's great.

EMILY

She's very nice.

MIA

Yes, she is.

EMILY

But she's a bit unusual.

MIA

Yes, she is.

EMILY

Do you know her well?

MIA

Yes, very well.

EMILY

What does she do?

MIA

Well... uh... Emily, can I trust you?

EMILY

Of course, you can. We're best friends, aren't we?

MIA

Can I tell you a secret and you promise you won't tell anyone?

EMILY

Sure. That's what friends are for.

MIA

Okay.

EMILY

Is it about you and Tom?

MIA

No, it's about Scarlet, my neighbor.

EMILY

What about her?

MIA

She isn't from here.

EMILY

I thought so. She has kind of an accent. What country is she from?

MIA

I mean, she isn't from the earth.

EMILY

What are you talking about?

MIA

She's from outer space.

EMILY

What? You mean like Mars or Jupiter?

MIA

Even further away.

EMILY

You're kidding.

MIA

No, it's the truth.

EMILY

And what's she doing here?

MIA

She is supposed to find a new home for her family.

EMILY

Do they want to move to the earth?

MIA

Yes, because their planet is dying.

EMILY

Don't you think we should tell the police about it? I mean, if they really are aliens, they might be dangerous.

MIA

I'm sure they aren't dangerous, Emily. And you promised you wouldn't tell anybody. You said I can trust you.

EMIILY

Yeah, sure, Mia. But what if they come here with an army of aliens and take over the earth and kill us all?

(Mia puts her left hand on Emily's right shoulder.)

MIA

Don't worry, Emily. Everything will be fine.

EMILY

I'm sorry, Mia, but I think we should at least tell our parents.

MIA *(gazes into Emily's eyes)*

May this secret be silent forever.

(Emily's whole body shakes for a moment.)

EMILY

Well, I guess I have to go home now. I'll pick you up for school tomorrow at eight.

MIA

Say Emily, can I trust you?

EMILY

Of course, you can. We're best friends, aren't we?

MIA

Can I tell you a secret and you promise you won't tell anyone?

EMILY

Sure. That's what friends are for.

MIA

Okay.

EMILY

Is it about you and Tom?

MIA

No, it's about Scarlet, my neighbor.

EMILY

Who's that? You've never told me about her before.

MIA

It isn't important. I'll tell you about her tomorrow.

EMILY

Okay, see you then.

(Emily leaves.)

MIA *(to the audience)*

Wow, she completely forgot what I told her.

(At that moment, Scarlet comes in.)

MIA

Scarlet, you're back already? I'm sorry, but I haven't had time to feed your Boogalooga yet.

SCARLET

That's okay. It was a quick trip, so I can feed the Boogalooga myself.

MIA

Did you see Emily?

SCARLET

Yes, I did, but she didn't seem to remember me. Did you tell her the secret?

MIA

Yes, I did, but I was afraid she might not be able to keep the secret.

SCARLET

So you put your left hand on her right shoulder and said: "May this secret be silent forever"?

MIA

Right. I said it, and it worked. She completely forgot what I told her about you.

SCARLET

That's good. You know, some secrets are just too hard to keep, so it can be good to make a secret into a secret again.

MIA

Thanks, Scarlet. I think I'll keep our secret a secret from now on.

SCARLET

So, can I trust you?

(Scarlet and Mia laugh.)

MIA
That's what neighbors are for, right?
SCARLET
Friends.
MIA
What?
SCARLET
That's what friends are for.
(Scarlet and Mia smile at each other.)

SCENE 4 DON'T WORRY

(Andrew and Christopher sit on opposite sides of the stage, facing the audience. Andrew dials a number on his cell phone. Christopher's phone rings.)

CHRISTOPHER *(picks up his phone)*

Hi, this is Chris. Is that you, Andy?

ANDREW *(shouting into the phone)*

I hate you!

(Andrew hangs up.)

CHRISTOPHER

Wait, Andrew, don't hang up! Andrew! Andy!

(Christopher puts his phone down. At that moment his older brother Hunter comes into the room and notices that something is wrong.)

HUNTER

Hey Chris, what's up? It looks like you just lost your best friend.

(Christopher nods.)

CHRISTOPHER

Yeah, I think I did.

HUNTER

Andrew?

CHRISTOPHER

Yeah.

HUNTER

What happened?

CHRISTOPHER

We were playing soccer at school.

HUNTER

On the playground?

CHRISTOPHER

Yeah.

HUNTER

There's nothing wrong with that.

CHRISTOPHER *(suddenly angry)*

But then he cheated!

HUNTER

Andrew?

CHRISTOPHER

Yeah.

HUNTER

How did he cheat?

CHRISTOPHER

He picked up the ball with his hands.

HUNTER

Was he the goalkeeper?

CHRISTOPHER

No, he wasn't.

HUNTER

So why did he pick up the ball?

CHRISTOPHER

'cause he said I fouled him.

HUNTER

And did you foul him?

CHRISTOPHER

I just bumped into him a bit and he fell on the ground. It was no big deal.

HUNTER

What happened then?

CHRISTOPHER

He got up and grabbed the ball, and yelled at me.

HUNTER

What did he say?

CHRISTOPHER

He said I knocked him down on purpose, and I told him I was just going after the ball. And then he called me a liar and said he got a free kick, 'cause I fouled him.

HUNTER

Did you foul him?

CHRISTOPHER

I just pushed him a little bit. It was nothing. I mean soccer's no game for babies.

HUNTER

Did you call him a baby?

CHRISTOPHER

Sure, I did!

HUNTER

And what did he do?

CHRISTOPHER

He put the ball down and started to take a free kick.

HUNTER

And what did you do?

CHRISTOPHER

I picked up the ball and called him a cheater.

HUNTER

And what did he do?

CHRISTOPHER

He walked away and didn't talk to me again all day. Except for now.

HUNTER

So that was Andrew on the phone?

CHRISTOPHER

Yeah.

HUNTER

What did he say?

CHRISTOPHER
He said he hated me and hung up.
HUNTER
Do you think he really hates you?
CHRISTOPHER
I don't know.
HUNTER
Do you hate him?
CHRISTOPHER
No way. He's my best friend. We do everything together. We talk about everything. I know all about him, and he knows all about me.
HUNTER
So what are you going to do?
CHRISTOPHER
I'm going to wait by the phone until he calls up again.
HUNTER
Why don't you call him?
CHRISTOPHER
No way! He hates me.
HUNTER
Does he really hate you? Or did he just say he hated you?
CHRISTOPHER
What's the difference?
HUNTER
Sometimes people say stuff they don't mean. But it's hard to take something back that you didn't mean.
CHRISTOPHER
So you don't think he hates me?
HUNTER
I'm sure he doesn't hate you.

CHRISTOPHER
Really?
HUNTER
Really. Why don't you give him a call and ask if he still wants to go to Jump Center this weekend.
CHRISTOPHER
You think it's okay to call him?
HUNTER
I know it's okay.
(Hunter walks off stage. Christopher picks up his phone and dials a number. Andrew's phone rings.)
ANDREW *(first looks at his phone, then answers it)*
This is Andrew speaking.
CHRISTOPHER
Andy, this is Chris.
ANDREW
Hi.
CHRISTOPHER
I'm sorry I called you a baby and a cheater.
ANDREW
Yeah?
CHRISTOPHER
And I wanted to know…
ANDREW
I'm sorry, too.
CHRISTOPHER
For what?
ANDREW
For calling you a liar.
CHRISTOPHER
That's okay. You were right to be angry when I knocked you down.

ANDREW

I know you didn't do it on purpose.

CHRISTOPHER

No, it was an accident. You know how wild I get when I play soccer.

ANDREW

Yeah, I remember the time you were so busy dribbling the ball that you ran into the goal post and got a concussion.

CHRISTOPHER

But I still played until the end of the match.

ANDREW

You really are crazy sometimes.

(Both boys laugh a bit. A pause.)

CHRISTOPHER

Are we still friends?

ANDREW

Sure.

CHRISTOPHER

And you don't hate me?

ANDREW

No way.

CHRISTOPHER

Are we still going to Jump Center this weekend together with my brother?

ANDREW

Of course. And afterwards you can sleep at my house and we can watch "Star Wars, the Rise of Skywalker" in our new cinema room.

CHRISTOPHER

Cool. I'll wear my Darth Vader costume.

ANDREW

And I'll wear my new Chewbacca costume!

CHRISTOPHER
Cool. See you tomorrow, Andy.
ANDREW
See you tomorrow, Chris.

SCENE 5   DON'T DO IT

(Dixie – with a large bag hanging from her shoulder – and Tara are walking in front of the audience. The audience is like a big department store where you can buy lots of things, so when Dixie "picks up something" at the department store – a CD, a phone, a sweatshirt – she reaches out towards the audience and acts like she is taking something from a rack or a shelf or a bin.)

DIXIE *(pointing at something in the audience ("department store")*

Look at all those CDs, Tara. Aren't they cool? I'd love to have millions of CDs, so I could listen to everything I want to listen to whenever I want to listen to it.

TARA

You don't need to buy CDs anymore, Dixie. CDs are old-school.

DIXIE

What do you mean?

TARA

My parents are selling all their CDs now, because they have Spotify.

DIXIE

Yeah, sure, my two brothers have Spotify, too, and they're always talking about their playlists of the week.

TARA

It's awesome. There are billions of songs you can listen to.

DIXIE

But I don't want billions of songs. I just want hundreds of CDs.

(Dixie "spots a CD" and takes it out of a rack.)

DIXIE

Like this one by Billie Eilish with "No Time to Die".

TARA

But you don't need to buy the CD. With Spotify you just pick the song and listen to it.

DIXIE *(holds up the imaginary CD)*

But I want the CD.

TARA

How are you going to buy it? You don't have any money.

DIXIE *(looks to the left, then to the right, then she puts the imaginary CD in her bag)*

Like this.

TARA *(gets very nervous)*

What are you doing, Dixie? You can't just take it.

DIXIE

Why not?

TARA

That's shoplifting.

DIXIE

Who cares? Everybody does it.

TARA

Have you ever done it before?

DIXIE

Lots of times. It's a real kick.

(Dixie moves further to the right and looks at "something" else in the audience.)

Wow, Tara, look at those new phones!

TARA

Don't do it, Dixie.

DIXIE *(looking at the "phones")*

Do what? I'm just looking.

TARA

You can get in lots of trouble..

DIXIE

No big deal. And anyway, I won't get caught.

TARA

They'll call the police, and your parents will have to come and pick you up.

DIXIE *("picking up a phone" and looking at "it")*

Oh, look at this Samsung Galaxy S10. I love the color.

TARA

Don't do it, Dixie.

DIXIE

Do what, Tara?

TARA

Don't steal the phone.

DIXIE

I'm not stealing it, Tara. I'm just looking at it.

(Dixie acts like she is trying out the phone. She pushes imaginary buttons, looks at the imaginary display, listens to imaginary ringtones – she could also sing the ringtones.)

TARA

Stop it, Dixie. Put it back. You're going to get both of us in trouble.

(Dixie looks to the left, then to the right, then she puts the imaginary phone in her bag)

TARA

Don't do it, Dixie, please!

(Dixie moves further to the right and looks at "something" else in the audience.)

DIXIE

Fantastic. Look at these hooded sweatshirts, Tara. They are so cool.

TARA *(nervous)*

Don't do it, Dixie. Those are Gucci Loopback hoodies. They cost over 1,000 dollars.

DIXIE *("taking a hoodie" from the "shelf")*
Who cares about money?
(Dixie holds up the imaginary hooded sweatshirt, smiles and stuffs "it" into her bag.)
TARA *(nervously looks around)*
Hey Dixie, I think someone is watching us.
DIXIE
No way. I never get caught. I have eyes in the back of my head.
(At that moment, a punk girl walks over to Dixie. It's L.A., Dixie's guardian angel.)
L.A. *(puts her head up close to Dixie, as if she wanted to whisper something in her ear)*
Cool bag.
(L.A. takes the bag from Dixie's shoulder and starts looking at the "things" inside.)
Wow, look at this. A Billie Eilish CD with that new James Bond song, "No Time to Cry".
DIXIE
"Die."
L.A. *(looks at Dixie, surprised)*
What?
DIXIE
"No Time to Die"!
L.A.
Whatever.
(L.A. continues to look at the "things" in the bag.)
DIXIE *(holding out her hand)*
Excuse me, that's my bag. Can I have it back, please?
L.A. *(ignoring Dixie)*
Oh, how cool. A new Samsung Galaxy S10. But the color is terrible.

DIXIE

It's my favorite color.

L.A. *(gives her a crazy look)*

You're kidding? That's your favorite color?

DIXIE

Yeah, it matches the hoodie I got.

L.A. *(looks inside the bag again)*

Oh yeah. A Gucci hoodie in pretty pink.

DIXIE *(Dixie grabs the bag)*

What's wrong with that?

TARA *(very nervous)*

I don't like this situation, Dixie. I'm leaving.

L.A. *(to Tara)*

Not so fast, kiddo. I'm not through with you girls yet.

TARA

What do you mean? Who are you?

L.A.

I'm L.A., Dixie's guardian angel.

DIXIE

My what?

L.A.

Your guardian angel. I'm here to make sure you don't do anything stupid.

TARA *(scared)*

I told her not to do it! I told her not to steal that stuff! I kept saying, "Don't do it, Dixie", but she wouldn't listen to me.

L.A.

Take it easy. Just calm down. I'm an angel and not a store detective. I'm L.A. from L.A., the city of angels.

TARA

Los Angeles? The city of angels? Cool.

L.A.

Yeah.

TARA

Awesome, L.A., where all the cool people live.

L.A.

Yeah, lots of cool people. But lots of cold hearts.

DIXIE

Cold-hearted cool people? That's so stupid.

L.A.

But not as stupid as shoplifting.

DIXIE

Who said I was shoplifting?

L.A.

Nobody said you were shoplifting.

DIXIE

Then what are you talking about?

L.A.

The stuff in your bag.

DIXIE

What about the stuff in my bag?

L.A.

It isn't yours.

DIXIE

Who says?

L.A.

Nobody.

DIXIE

Then how do you know I didn't already pay for the stuff?

L.A.

I know everything about you, what you do, what you think, what you feel.

DIXIE

Oh yeah, wise guy? So what do I feel now?

L.A.

Scared.

DIXIE

And what am I thinking?

L.A.

You're thinking of dropping your bag and running.

DIXIE

That's right.

TARA

How did you know that?

L.A.

Like I said, I'm Dixie's guardian angel.

TARA

And you're here to keep her from doing something stupid?

L.A.

Exactly. I'm like her best friend.

DIXIE

Tara's my best friend.

TARA

Yeah, I'm Dixie's best friend.

L.A.

I'm not her best friend, I'm just like her best friend, because I only want the best for her.

TARA

Just like me.

L.A.

Exactly. *(starting to walk away – over her shoulder)* And what does a best friend do, Tara?

TARA

She helps out when her friend is in trouble.

L.A. *(walking away)*

Right, Tara. *(nodding at Dixie)* She's all yours.

TARA *(taking hold of Dixie's arm.)*

Come on, Dixie, I'll help you put the stuff back.

DIXIE

Thanks, Tara. *(looks at L.A.)* Thanks, L.A.

L.A.

That's what guardian angels are for, Dixie. Take care and be a good kid.

(L.A. walks off stage.)

TARA

And this is what friends are for.

(Tara puts her arm around Dixie's shoulder, and they walk off stage.)

SCENE 6   ME? JEALOUS?

(Harriet is sitting on a bench. Kenny walks over to her and sits down. He is very shy.)

KENNY

Hi, Harriet.

HARRIET

Hi.

(She gives him a funny look.)

Sorry, what was your name again?

KENNY *(surprised)*

Kenny.

HARRIET

Benny?

KENNY *(stressing the "K")*

Kenny.

HARRIET *(nodding)*

Right. Denny.

KENNY *(gives Harriet a funny look)*

Kenny!!

HARRIET

Oh yeah, Kenny. You're in my History class, aren't you?

KENNY *(once again surprised)*

No, I'm in your English class. I sit next to you.

HARRIET:

Oh yeah, now I remember.

KENNY *(changing the subject)*

You're new at school, aren't you?

HARRIET

Yeah.

KENNY

Where did you live before coming here?

HARRIET

New York City.

KENNY

A big city girl?

HARRIET

Yeah.

KENNY *(notices a ring on her finger)*

Nice ring.

HARRIET

What?

KENNY

Nice ring you have there.

(He points at it and almost touches it.)

HARRIET

Be careful.

KENNY

What?

HARRIET

Don't touch it.

KENNY

Okay… Do you like it here in this small town?

HARRIET

No.

KENNY

What don't you like?

HARRIET

The people.

KENNY

You mean the adults?

HARRIET

The adults, the kids, even the dogs and cats. I hate them all.

KENNY

What don't you like about them?

HARRIET

Boring.

KENNY

What?

HARRIET

They're all boring. Everybody's boring here.

KENNY

Like me?

HARRIET

Yeah.

KENNY

Would you like me to leave?

HARRIET

Yeah.

KENNY

Okay. *(getting up)* See you in English class.

HARRIET

Yeah. Whatever.

(While walking off stage, Kenny runs into his best friend Mac.)

MAC

Hey, Kenny. What are you doing here?

KENNY

I was just talking to that new girl, Harriet.

MAC

Oh yeah? Where is she?

KENNY

She's over there on the bench.

(Mac looks at Harriet on the bench.)

MAC:

Oh yeah. She's waiting for me.

(*Mac waves to Harriet, and she waves back.*)
KENNY
Oh yeah? She's really cute…
MAC
I think so, too.
KENNY
But she thinks everybody is boring.
MAC
Everybody except me.
KENNY
What do you mean?
MAC
Didn't I tell you? Harriet and I are going together.
KENNY
Since when?
MAC
Since yesterday.
KENNY
How did that happen?
MAC
I treated her to some ice cream, and then she said she liked me. So I gave her my ring.
KENNY
What for?
MAC
Because she likes me, and I like her.
KENNY
You like her?
MAC
Yeah, why not?
KENNY
She isn't very nice.

MAC

She's really nice to me.

KENNY

And you really gave her your ring?

MAC

Sure.

KENNY

That was stupid of you.

MAC

Hey, what's your problem? Are you jealous?

KENNY

Me? Jealous? No way.

MAC

You sure sound jealous.

(At that moment, Harriet gets up and walks towards the two boys.)

HARRIET

Hi, Mac. Hi, Benny.

MAC

Hi, sweetheart.

KENNY

Kenny.

MAC

What?

KENNY

My name's Kenny, not Benny.

MAC: *(to Harriet)*

You two know each other?

HARRIET

Yeah, sure. Denny sits next to me in History class.

KENNY

English.

MAC

What?

KENNY

She sits next to me in English, not History.

HARRIET

Whatever.

KENNY

And my name is Kenny.

HARRIET

Whatever.

MAC

Hey, Kenny. Don't you have your guitar lesson now?

KENNY

Yeah, but…

MAC *(to Kenny)*

See you later, dude. *(to Harriet)* Say, Harriet… Can I treat you to some ice cream?

HARRIET

I never say no to ice cream.

MAC

Then let's go!

(Mac and Harriet walk off stage. Kenny watches them go.)

KENNY

I'll call you later, Mac.

(No answer.)

SCENE 7   A JOLLY GOOD FELLOW

(Tony is sitting on a bench. He is staring into space. Three boys – Ethan, Jonathan and Cooper – walk past him. They stop at the side of the bench.)

ETHAN

Hi, Tony. How's it going?

(No reaction from Tony. Ethan, Jonathan and Cooper exchange looks.)

JONATHAN

I heard about what happened.

COOPER

Yeah, I really feel sorry for you, Tony.

(Tony looks at all three and nods. Then he goes on looking into space.)

ETHAN

Is there anything we can do for you, Tony?

(Tony shakes his head and looks down. The other boys exchange looks.)

JONATHAN

Okay, well, let us know if we can help you in any way…

COOPER

See you around, Tony.

(The three boys walk to the side of the stage and stop. They stand together and freeze their positions. Two boys – Mike and Ed – appear on the other side of the stage. They see Tony and walk over to him.)

MIKE

Hey, Tony. I haven't seen you for a couple of weeks.

ED

It's good to see you, buddy.

(Tony nods.)

MIKE

How's everything going?

(Tony shrugs his shoulders.)

ED

I guess things have been pretty tough for you since…

(Mike nudges Ed with his elbow to stop him from finishing his sentence. Tony looks up at Ed, pauses for a moment, then shakes his head and looks down again.)

MIKE

I saw your sister yesterday and talked to her a bit.

(Tony nods, still looking down.)

She told me how tough this is for you. And I thought, maybe Ed and me, maybe the three of us could do some stuff together, like last summer. You and me and Ed. Remember how we played tennis last summer?

(Tony looks up for a second, pauses, then shakes his head and looks down again.)

ED

It might be a bit too early to think about it, but if you feel like playing tennis with us, just give me a call.

MIKE

We know you can do it.

ED

You still have my number, don't you?

(Tony nods and looks away.)

MIKE

Okay, well, see you around, Tony.

ED:

Take care, Tony.

(Without looking up, Tony waves.)

MIKE

Just give us a call, okay?

(Mike and Ed walk over to Ethan, Jonathan and Cooper and freeze their positions as well. After a short pause, Tony looks over at the group of boys, then he lowers his head again and shakes it slowly. At that moment, five girls show up behind him – Sarah, Angelina, Ariane, Jackie and Pia. Tony doesn't turn around, but he seems to know they are there.)

SARAH

Listen, Tony. We want you to know that we're behind you all the way.

ANGELINA

No matter what happens, we'll always give you a helping hand.

ARIANE

You can count on us, Tony, because we're your friends.

JACKIE

Whenever you need us, just let us know.

PIA

You're one of the nicest boys at school.

SARAH

We understand how hard it is for you.

ANGELINA

We know it's very difficult to get used to a change like this.

ARIANE

But we know you can do it.

JACKIE

You're tough, you're smart, and you're really good-looking.

PIA:

There's nobody at school who doesn't like you.

SARAH:

Even my grandmother still talks about you. Remember when she used to pick us up from daycare and take us to the playground? "What a nice boy," she always says. "That's the boy you should marry, Sarah."

(Tony looks up for a moment. There's the hint of a smile on his face.)

ANGELINA

And we're also here, because we want to give you something.

ARIANE

We know how much you like music.

JACKIE

And that you're a great singer, too.

PIA

So we brought you this invitation.

SARAH *(handing Tony a piece of paper.)*

You know about our pitch perfect choir.

(Tony takes the piece of paper and starts reading.)

ANGELINA

We have a big concert in two weeks.

ARIANE

And we really need a voice like yours.

JACKIE

Please say yes. You won't regret it.

PIA

You'll love singing with all these beautiful girls.

ANGELINA

And we'd love to sing with you.

TONY *(clearing his voice, reading the invitation)*

"Dear Tony, we would be proud to have you join our pitch perfect choir. We need someone like you with a magical voice and real sound power."

(Tony looks at the invitation a bit longer. Everyone is silent. Then Tony looks up and nods. The five boys standing at the edge of the stage all shout.)

JONATHAN , ETHAN, COOPER, ED, MIKE
Yes!!
(All the girls begin to sing:)
SARAH, ANGELINA, ARIANE, JACKIE, PIA
(While they are singing, Tony's sister Taylor pushes a wheelchair in front of the bench. Ed and Mike come over and help her pick up Tony and put him on the wheelchair.)
For he's a jolly good fellow!
For he's a jolly good fellow!
For he's a jolly good fellow!
Which nobody can deny!
Which nobody can deny!
Which nobody can deny!
For he's a jolly good fellow!
For he's a jolly good fellow!
For he's a jolly good fellow!
Which nobody can deny…
(Everybody applauds as Taylor pushes Tony off stage.)

SCENE 8   YOU CAN DO IT

(Five students are standing in front of the audience – Victoria, Giselle, Courtney, Dave and Steve. They are yelling – over the heads of the audience - at someone who is apparently behind the audience.)

VICTORIA, GISELLE, COURTNEY, DAVE, STEVE

(Victoria is filming with her Smartphone, Giselle is timing the "event" with her Smartphone, Courtney, Dave and Steve are cupping their hands around their mouths, raising their fists, slowly looking upwards, as if they are watching someone climb up a rope)

C'mon, Rudolfo! Yeah! Yeah! You can do it! Keep going! Great! You're almost there! Faster! Don't give up!

RUDOLFO *(not visible, in the back, behind the audience)*

Aaaaahhhhhhh!

(We hear a big BOOM from the back.)

VICTORIA, GISELLE, COURTNEY, DAVE, STEVE

(disappointed)

Aaawwwwww!

VICTORIA

Are you okay, Rudolfo?

GISELLE

Rudolfo?

COURTNEY

Say something, Rudolfo. Are you still alive?

DAVE

Rudolfo!?

STEVE

Do you need any help, Rudolfo?

DAVE

No way, Steve. You know we're not supposed to help him?

COURTNEY

Yeah, the challenge won't count if we help him.

VICTORIA

He has to do it alone.

STEVE

Sorry, I'm just used to helping people.

GISELLE

Okay, we know you mean well, Steve, but this time Rudolfo has to do it alone. By the way, Rudolfo, your time was great.

COURTNEY

Rudolfo? Is everything all right?

RUDOLFO *(from behind the audience, not visible)*

Yeah, my bum hurts a bit, but I'm okay.

DAVE

Are you ready to try it again?

STEVE

Rudolfo? Are you ready?

RUDOLFO

Yeah. Just a sec. My hands are sweaty. I have to wipe them off.

VICTORIA

Let me know when you're ready.

RUDOLFO

I'll count down from five. 5, 4, 3, 2, 1…

VICTORIA

Action!

VICTORIA, GISELLE, COURTNEY, DAVE, STEVE

Go!

(Victoria is filming with her Smartphone, Giselle is timing the "event" with her Smartphone, Courtney, Dave and Steve are cupping their hands around their mouths, raising their fists, slowly looking upwards.)

C'mon, Rudolfo! Yeah! Yeah! You can do it! Keep going! Great! You're almost there! Faster! Don't give up!

(Everybody's eyes are still looking upwards.)

VICTORIA

Keep going, Rudolfo!

DAVE

Oh no, he's slowing down.

STEVE

How's the time, Vickie?

VICTORIA

He's still fast enough to break the school record, but if he goes any slower...

GISELLE

No, Rudolfo! Don't stop!

RUDOLFO

Aaaaahhhhhhh!

(We hear a big BOOM from the back.)

VICTORIA, GISELLE, COURTNEY, DAVE, STEVE

(disappointed)

Aaawwwww!

VICTORIA

Are you okay, Rudolfo?

GISELLE

Rudolfo?

COURTNEY

Say something, Rudolfo. Are you still alive?

DAVE

Rudolfo!?

COURTNEY

I think we should take a break. Rudolfo must be so tired.

STEVE

Do you need anything to drink, Rudolfo?

DAVE

No way, Steve. You know he isn't allowed to drink anything during the challenge.

COURTNEY

Yeah, the challenge won't count if he drinks something.

RUDOLFO

Sorry, guys. I think everything is okay now.

STEVE

Shall we try it again?

RUDOLFO

I'll count down from five. 5, 4, 3, 2, 1…

VICTORIA

Action!

VICTORIA, GISELLE, COURTNEY, DAVE, STEVE

Go!

(Victoria is filming with her Smartphone, Giselle is timing the "event" with her Smartphone, Courtney, Dave and Steve are cupping their hands around their mouth, raising their fists, slowly looking upwards.)

C'mon, Rudolfo! Yeah! Yeah! You can do it! Keep going! Great! You're almost there! Faster! Don't give up!

(Everybody's eyes stop looking upwards.)

VICTORIA

Keep going, Rudolfo!

GISELLE

Yes, yes, yes!

COURTNEY

He's really fast this time.

DAVE

It looks like he's going to break the record.

STEVE

How's his time, Giselle?

GISELLE

Faster than ever.

C'mon, Rudolfo! Yeah! Yeah! You can do it!

(We hear a bell, and everybody cheers.)

GISELLE

It's a new school record!

VICTORIA, GISELLE, COURTNEY, DAVE, STEVE

Hooray! You did it, Rudolfo!

(We see Rudolfo running to the stage. The others congratulate him.)

GISELLE *(to Rudolfo)*

You're the fastest rope climber in school history! Congratulations!

RUDOLFO

Hey guys, thanks for all your help. I never would have made it without you!

STEVE

Always glad to help a friend.

(Steve slaps Rudolfo on the back, and the whole group leaves the stage together.)

SCENE 9   I'M SORRY

(Lilly and Riley are standing at opposite sides of the stage. They slowly start walking towards each other, threateningly, like gunfighters in a Western. They walk past each other without slowing down, but after about six feet (two meters), they both stop – with their backs to each other. A few seconds later, they turn their heads and exchange looks.)

LILLY

Riley…

(Lilly turns completely and starts to walk towards Riley, but Riley turns her head away and walks off stage. Lilly watches her go, then she turns to face the audience.)

LILLY

I don't know what to do. Riley and me… *(nodding in the direction Riley left)* We're best friends. I mean, we were best friends. And then something happened. She told me a secret, and I promised I wouldn't tell anybody else, but you know how it is sometimes? I was having a nice time with Johanna, and I just felt really cool, 'cause I knew Riley's secret, so I told Johanna – I told her Riley's secret… Excuse me?

(She acts like someone in the audience asked her about the secret.)

LILLY

No. No way. I'm not going to tell you Riley's secret. It was bad enough that I told Johanna, and she told Riley that she knew her secret, and Riley told me that she never wanted to talk to me again.

(Suddenly Dakota and Jamey appear on stage. They walk towards Lilly.)

DAKOTA

Hey, Lilly. Is it true what we heard about Riley?

LILLY

What did you hear about Riley?

JAMEY

Johanna told us that Riley was at Armstrong's Department Store and she got caught…

LILLY

Shh! Quiet! Somebody might hear us.

DAKOTA

Hey, what's the problem? If Johanna knows, everybody knows.

JAMEY

Yeah, the whole school is talking about it.

DAKOTA

And we thought you could tell us the details.

JAMEY

Since you and Riley are best friends.

LILLY

Not anymore.

DAKOTA

Oh yeah? Why not?

JAMEY

What happened?

LILLY

Riley told me her secret and asked me not to tell anybody else.

JAMEY

But you told Johanna, didn't you?

DAKOTA

The biggest blabbermouth at school.

LILLY

And she probably told everybody about it.

DAKOTA

She sure did.

JAMEY

And now everybody knows Riley's secret, because you broke your promise?

LILLY

Right.

JAMEY

Not good.

I know. I feel really sorry about it.

DAKOTA

Then why don't you apologize to Riley?

LILLY

I tried to, but she won't listen.

JAMEY

Well, keep trying to talk to her. You don't want to lose a friend like her.

LILLY

That's for sure. Thanks, Jamey.

DAKOTA

And remember: Keep every promise you make, and only make promises you can keep.

LILLY

You're so right. Take care, Dakota. See you around, Jamey.

(Jamey and Dakota walk off stage.)

LILLY *(once again talking to the audience)*

I feel so stupid. I really don't understand why I broke my promise and told Riley's secret to Johanna. I wish I could put everything right again.

(At that moment, Tom and Jason appear at the side of the stage.)

TOM

Hey, Lilly, did you hear about that rumor?

LILLY

What rumor?

JASON

The rumor about Riley at Armstrong's Department Store?

LILLY

What about it?

TOM

Fake news. She didn't get caught for shoplifting at Armstrong's.

LILLY

What?

JASON

Yeah, it was all just a rumor somebody made up.

LILLY

You're kidding!

TOM

No, it's true. Riley said she hasn't been to Armstrong's for ages.

LILLY

Oh yeah? That's good to know. Thanks, guys.

JASON

Sure thing, Lilly. See you around.

TOM

See you, Lilly.

LILLY

Take care, guys.

(Lilly turns to the audience again.)

LILLY

I don't believe it! Does that mean what Riley told me is fake? She wasn't caught shoplifting at Armstrong's?

(At that moment, Riley appears at the side of the stage and starts walking towards Lilly.)

RILEY

Lilly, I wanted to say I'm sorry.

LILLY

Riley, what are you doing here?

RILEY

I wanted to say I'm sorry.

LILLY

For what?

RILEY

For telling you a lie.

LILLY

What do you mean?

RILEY

The secret I told you… it was a lie, fake, not true.

LILLY

You mean you didn't get caught shoplifting at Armstrong's?

RILEY

No, I didn't. I've never done any shoplifting anywhere.

LILLY

So why did you tell me the fake secret?

RILEY

To test you.

LILLY

And I failed.

RILEY

Not really. I saw that it's difficult to keep a juicy secret like I told you. And maybe it's better not to tell your best friend the juiciest secret.

LILLY

Because you can't trust me?

RILEY

Because it's difficult to keep something so juicy secret.

LILLY
Does that mean we're still friends?
RILEY
Silly girl. You'll always be my best friend.
LILLY
Thanks, Riley.
RILEY
You bet, Lilly.
(The two girls hug.)

ABOUT THE AUTHOR

John Reed Middleton was born in Cedar Rapids, Iowa (USA). He was a teacher for 43 years at a German school in Hamburg where he taught English, Drama and Art. He has also spent over 35 years subtitling films and translating screenplays (www.middleton-group-translations.com).
During the past 30 years he has performed his own five one-act plays (DAVID, THE DEATH OF A CLOWN, CARNIVAL AT CASTLE ROCK, KILLING DADDY, LITTLE GOETHE and DAS KLEID) at small theaters in and around Hamburg.

THE PLAYLET SERIES is his latest writing project, topical collections of scenes in English for English learners from Year 1 to Year 12 (Level 1 to Level 6) who want to perform (english-playlets.com).

By purchasing the play, you automatically obtain the stage rights.